MW01593248

Maintain Happiness
Uplift your spirits during lockdown. Shift your power into happiness
– created with a mother's heart.

Lynnie R. Ceniza

Maintain Happiness

Introduction

Life has many ups and downs - it is how we cope with them that reveals our character. It can be difficult to change and take charge on our own - we often need the help of others.
I wanted to share with you the way I think about life and its problems, and the way I have learned to address my problems. Sometimes, all we need is a nudge from a good friend to set us going in the right direction - with confidence and a stronger belief in myself.
Writing this piece has helped me to formulate my plans and goals. We should try to remember that every day we should work to get a little closer to our goals as well.

CONTENTS

Introduction

1   Are you chasing the elusive butterfly of happiness? p.1

2   Are you worried? 4 steps to peace of mind.   p.5

3   Positive steps to discover the purpose of life.   p.8

4   Acceptance.   p.12

5   Secrets of a Positive Attitude.   p.17

6   Surprisingly quick and easy ways to feel happier.   p.22

7   Creating your underlying principle.   p.27

8   A gift of energy.   p.36

9   Appreciate yourself and what you have.   p.45

Maintain Happiness

1 ARE YOU CHASING THE ELUSIVE BUTTERFLY OF HAPPINESS?

For many people happiness is an elusive butterfly in the garden of life. Imagine a young child in the garden on a summer day. The child sees a beautiful butterfly flitting from flower to flower. With eyes of wonder the child wants to see it close up, touch it, and hold it in their hands. The child goes towards the flower that the butterfly is resting on, with arms outstretched, only to find as he just gets in reach, the butterfly moves to another flower. Undeterred the child follows the butterfly to the next flower, and then the next, but the butterfly always stays just out of reach.

As adults, happiness can seem just like that butterfly, always just out of reach. It becomes almost an obsession and the words "if only…" become an increasingly large part of our thoughts and vocabulary. If only I had more money I would be happy, if only I was in a great relationship I would be happy, if only I could have a different job……….and the list goes on. Even if we achieve one of our "if only "desires, the happiness we seek is still just out of our reach. The truth of the saying "The grass is always greener on the other side of the fence" becomes our focus and perception. If this becomes our focus, we find that dissatisfaction and unhappiness increasingly keep growing in our life and experience.

The unhappiness within us cannot be completely satisfied by external events or circumstances. To find happiness in life we must first be at peace with ourselves internally. External events and circumstances can bring us happiness in the moment, but they do not have a lasting effect on our inner self. Life experience brings a mixture of good and bad circumstances to everyone. To rely on life's experiences for our source of happiness would mean living life in a constant emotional roller coaster ride.

Happiness comes from within. The inner contentment that survives the roller coaster ride of life has its roots deep within our being. The source of happiness comes from finding and embracing who we are as a person, and living a life of purpose. We need to find peace in every aspect of our life- the physical, mental, emotional and spiritual. To discover acceptance, purpose and peace in all of these areas will give a sense of completion in life. If we neglect any one of these areas, we experience a sense of emptiness and feel something is missing. There is not a solid foundation for building happiness within, but we then typically start to try to fill this incompleteness by looking for outside solutions. That is the point when we can fall into the 'elusive butterfly' syndrome, and experience such frustration.

Is happiness an elusive butterfly for you? Spend some time in quiet reflection. Are you neglecting one of the four important parts of who you are and experiencing a sense of emptiness within? The more you discover, embrace and accept your uniqueness and purpose, the more you will experience the butterfly of happiness alighting on your shoulder.

2 ARE YOU WORRIED? HERE ARE 4 STEPS TO PEACE OF MIND

A friend has this quotation on his office wall: "I know worry works because nothing I worry about ever happens."

I think I must believe that, because I worry a lot -- and about the most insignificant things. I worry about the big things, of course, like health, relationships, and finances. But I'm also liable to fret about anything and everything that finds its way into my consciousness.

Because I spend so much time on worry, I've decided to embrace it with a personal research project. Maybe you'd like to join me.

Here are two avenues I'm exploring:

1) I practice catching myself at it. "Hey, I'm worrying again." During a recent morning swim, I caught myself worrying 10 times during one lap! I'm not kidding. On rare days when I don't have anything to worry about, I find something. What I've learned is that worry is a mental habit. I can change habits; I've done it before. There's hope.

2) My second approach is to practice presence. By this I mean stopping my thoughts. In my workshops, I ring a bell to help participants practice centering. The quieter we are, the longer we hear the bell. There's a lovely moment when we all listen . . . until the ring is barely audible . . . then just a memory. I relish that moment of quiet before my thoughts re-engage. There is no future or past, just Now. No worrying thoughts -- no thoughts at all. It's a peaceful place, which is why I stretch the moment. I want to strengthen the connection to something greater than my worries.

3) When I told my good friend Rosie about my worry project, she told me about her approach, which is to do one of three things: decide to address the issue right then; if you can't do anything about it at the moment, give yourself a time to address it later; or decide that it is not important and let it go. In other words, act on it, file it or throw it away.

4) Finally, one of Rosie's favorite worry stoppers (and mine) is to sing. Connect with yourself, your creativity, and the place where everything really is okay.

Awareness and acknowledgment are the keys to changing our habits. Morihei Ueshiba, who founded aikido and spoke of it as the Art of Peace, said we must "always practice the Art of Peace in a vibrant and joyful manner." Perhaps my research project on worry will help me to lighten up, smile, and live each day in such a way.

Are you worrying? Stop your thoughts for a moment. Listen to the sounds around you, pay attention, and be present to this key moment. And smile . . . for no reason. You may find that's the best reason of all.

3 POSITIVE STEPS TO DISCOVER THE PURPOSE OF LIFE

If your life is not as passionate as you would like it to be, if you lack the zest and energy for living, it is because you lack an underlying principle around which one's life should be organized.

The process of discovering this underlying principle may be the most powerful thing you will ever do yourself, because it will give your life a direction, a purpose. It will provide you with the clarity and focus that could awaken the unbelievable forces hidden somewhere deep inside you.

In this article we will discuss the concept of life and its underlying principle. We will be going through a step by step procedure, exploring your feelings and options, and by the end of this article, you should have a fairly solid tool you could immediately employ in your life, to give it a meaningful direction.

There are three steps to the process of discovering the purpose of your life:

Understanding the principle of choice

Creating your underlying principle

Aligning your life with the underlying principle

Understanding the principle of choice

Norman Vincent Peale has this to say about the power of choice. "The greatest power we have is the power of choice. It is an actual fact, that if you have been drowning under unhappiness, you can choose to be joyous, instead. And, by effort, lift yourself into joy. If you tend to be fearful, you can overcome that misery by choosing to have courage. The whole trend and the quality of anyone's life is determined by the choices that are made".

Choosing is the most important activity of your mind, because by making a choice, you are proclaiming your desires to your subconscious mind. Once the subconscious mind gets to know your desires, it is going to do anything to manifest them in your life. The choices you make in your life become your goal. And, if you are sincere in pursuing them, there is no reason why you should not accomplish them.

Indecision, on the other hand, not only creates frustration and anxiety, but can also confuse the subconscious mind about what you want. But it is important that the choices you make are made by you, in accordance with your true desires, purposes and attitude. A lot of us let others make choices for us, or make our choices according to what we think is 'correct', even if that means that we go against our wishes. What is right for someone else may not be right for you, and the way to know this is listening to what your heart says.

So, begin with, make a list of things which interests you; things which you have always enjoyed, which makes you feel better, which inspires you to surge ahead, no matter what obstacles you face. Do you like doing something creative, or something artistic? Do you enjoy nature, do you like the sea? Do you enjoy helping others? Do you get pleasure out of making a difference in other people's life?

Whatever it is that interests you, go ahead and make a list under the following headlines:

Things you love to do:

_____

_____

_____

_____

What is it that you love in these things and why? How could you do this for money, and make a living out of it?

_____

_____

_____

_____

_____

4 ACCEPTANCE

I was first thinking , when exactly does one start to yearn for acceptance?

Is it when we are born?

Is it when we first feel the pain of non-acceptance?

Is it when we begin to be challenged in sports?

Is it when we fall into the ever talked about `peer pressure`?

Is it when we fall in love?

Is it when we start a new job?

Is it when we become a new member of a family?

Is it when we move to a new city or country?

Is it when we write our very first book?

I believe it is all of the above.When people feel the need to be accepted, they will do leaps and bounds to succeed in this quest.

Athletes and bodybuilders will take drugs to win. Winning = acceptance.

When we fall in love , our entire being wants to feel accepted by our mate.

Authors will spend hours and hours to write the exact words to please their readers and go to great lengths to publish their creation.

Becoming a new member of a family whether it be through marriage or adoption will create a need to be nurtured as one who genuinely belongs.

Starting a new job is a definite acceptance need, we need to fit in so we can relax and apply ourselves 100% to our job.

Moving to a new country or city or even just a new neighbourhood, is very challenging for us and to be accepted and fit in, is a very important step in our settling in.

Let's not forget Peer Pressure, that's a tough one, children just getting started in high school suffer the most with this one, hormones are swinging and their emotions are so sensitive. The fears that they have struggled with for the year before is all up front and they have a whole lot of reality to deal with. To fit in and be accepted by their peers is more than half the battle.

Being a baby has a world of need to be accepted and see our parents smile when we please them.

The pain of non-acceptance for the first time cuts like a knife. It wounds us for life, creating a scar that we grow with forever.

All these worries, needs and desires are in all of us that live and breathe. Some of us feel the hunger for acceptance less than others. Some of us cannot live without acceptance, we become obsessed in our thinking, trying anything we can to fit in.

Do you read the words "self esteem" in anything I have written here today? You should do it because it is in every sentence. The need for acceptance somehow affects our self-esteem which in turns affects our emotional and mental stability, where jealousy, worry and anxiety seed from. If you are familiar with the feeling of non-acceptance or low self-esteem, then you must be aware how controlled you are by the worry that follows them and how much of your life is imprisoned by that other mind.

Low self-esteem and non-acceptance are exactly what they seem, 'another mind' and one can actually feel them at war within ourselves. It reminds me of the good devil and bad devil scenario. Trust me here, it is no fun at all for the person that is imprisoned by it, not only do they have to balance the two minds, but they also have the guilt that they feel when they see what the result of the battle in their heads is doing to the people around them, people they love. The constant questions that one faces, as in my blog FEELINGS!!!! are an added, and excruciating pain to the already lonely tortured person.

So if anyone out there knows a person that suffers from non-acceptance or low self-esteem, HUG them and please try to have more patience and understand that they are not having a picnic and that if just saying , "stop it" or "just don`t think about it" could stop it, they would in a heartbeat. We all need support and acceptance to get us through our lows. Kicking someone when they are down, never ever helps them to get up.

I am doing what I can through my website and my blog to help educate people and help them understand what low self-esteem is all about and how very intense and serious it is.

5 SECRETS OF A POSITIVE ATTITUDE

Are you constantly bombarded by thoughts of negativity? Plagued by feelings of insecurity? Do you see everything in a negative manner? The reason for this lies deep within your heart. You are what you mentally and spiritually eat. If a person drinks alcohol on a daily basis, odds are their body will be affected in some way. They may have liver issues, develop cancer or incur some other type of health problem directly related to the amount of alcohol they have consumed. It is very likely they will die young unless they do something about it. In the same way, a person who constantly feeds themselves negative thoughts will simply turn into a negative person.

This is the time to go on a diet. Not a normal food diet, but a diet of positive attitude food. You have to literally stop feeding your mind negative things. Whenever you have a thought, ask yourself, is this thought positive or negative? What do negative thoughts look like? Well, they start with 'can''t rather than 'can', 'no' as opposed to 'yes', and 'will' and not 'won't'. The Bible, which is the greatest, and most powerful, self help book ever written, speaks about taking every thought captive. The problem in our society has become that our thoughts have taken us captive. We have begun to let our thoughts control us.

A great way to know what we are feeling negative about is to ask those people who are closest to us. You can ask your spouse or another person in your life who really knows you how they would rate your attitude on a scale of 1 to 10. 10 being super positive and 1 being super negative. Ask this person to be totally honest with you. You will benefit from their honesty even if it causes you some pain. Ask this person what it is that you specifically say that they perceive as being negative. Write down what they tell you and look at the actual words. Now is the time to be brutally honest with yourself. Those words are a reflection of what is inside you. They are who you are. The great thing is that you can change. It is as simple as making a choice to do so. You must consciously decide to replace the thoughts of negativity with thoughts of positivity.

Decide what positive words you will change the negative words written on your paper to. Once you have done this, make an effort to insert these new positive thoughts in your mind. You will soon begin to notice a positive change taking place in your life. Your family, friends and co-workers will all notice it as well. They may not know what is different about you. But they will know that you are not the same person that you were. They will see this as an improvement, this should help with your self-esteem.

The items which are causing negativity in your life could very well be the news, movies, constantly replaying tragedy in your mind and the list could go on. These things should be eliminated if you want your new mental health regimen to be a success. The news is always very negative and does not help someone who is trying to rid their mind of such thoughts.at all. When you are feeding yourself thoughts of death from a war or gunshot or car accident visually the outcome will be negative. I do believe there is a time to grieve over the death of a loved one.

However, if a person constantly replays this negative event in their minds it can lead to further depression. If you are grieving, the person who has passed away is not coming back and we must close that chapter in our lives and move on to the next chapter. This is a difficult task which can only be done by making a decision to proceed with our own life, no matter how hard this may be.

You can do it. You can and will have a positive attitude, if you simply take the steps outlined above. It will get easier as you get used to it. You do not have to be what you were in the past. You can be different in the future. The choice is yours. I know you will make a positive one.

6 SURPRISINGLY QUICK AND EASY WAYS TO FEEL HAPPIER

All of us have days when we're out of sorts. You just wish you were in a better mood. You've had days like that, haven't you? Perhaps you tried to get yourself into a better state of mind but struggled to achieve it. It is difficult at first, but it is possible.

Sometimes we get stuck in our own emotional dumps and forget how easy it is to feel happier, so here are seven simple ways to lift your mood. Many people have found them useful. Some of them may surprise you!

1. Go for a walk.

Most people know that going for a short daily walk is one of the best forms of exercise. When you are feeling down it is even more beneficial. If you can, go into a natural environment with plants and birds. AWay from lots of people.. It will be more relaxing, and ease your mind. Can you think of such a setting? What do you notice first? The different shades of greenery, the fresh smell of country air, the sounds of birds, or the sunlight shining through the trees? Make it real by taking a short stroll.

2. Listen to quality music.

Music can shift a listener's state within moments. It's effect can be nearly magical. Dig out that CD you haven't listened to in ages or tune in your radio to something you've never listened to before. Classical music is particularly restful and beneficial.

3. Open yourself to discovering something new.

Read something (printed, not on line) different from what you would normally read. There are a ton of different types of magazines and you can get these days. Visit your local library or browse through a magazine rack. Pick up or buy a magazine you wouldn't normally buy. You may discover something wonderful. If you lack the concentration to read, try listening to an audiobook.

4. Find something to laugh at.

Laughter is one of the best ways to lift your spirits. Find a humorous book, or watch a comedy. Even better, try to learn a few new jokes and tell them to others. We all have a sense of humor, but sometimes it gets hidden and it takes practice to bring it out again.

5. Simple breathing meditation.

Breathing meditation is a great exercise that you can do anywhere. Simply allow yourself to sit comfortably with your back straight.

Now close your eyes and become aware of the flow of air into and out of your nostrils. Breathe deeply and slowly. That's all there is to it. Do this for 10-15 minutes whenever you feel anxious. Notice how pleasantly surprised you can be at how you feel afterward.

6. Doodling for the fun of it.

Most people can remember when they were young and used to doodle for hours. Kids love drawing silly little pictures. Drawing is not just for kids or artists. Whoever you are, get some pens, pencils, crayons or whatever you have and just draw for the fun of it. Notice how your state of mind shifts.

7. Think of others less fortunate.

The fact that you are reading this article suggests that you are probably much better off than most people on this planet. At times this may be hard to believe, but if you can read and have access to the internet, just those two things alone means you are better off than two thirds of all the people in the world. There are many human beings that barely have access to the basics of survival, waking up hungry more often than not. There are people in lots of pain. Allow your compassion for them to grow.

These are all pretty simple. There's nothing profound or life changing, but when all you need is a quick pick me up, these may be just the thing you need. Putting simple ideas, methods, tools and techniques into action will help you achieve change more quickly and easily--surprisingly so at times-- than you imagine.

7 CREATING YOUR UNDERLYING PRINCIPLE

The next step is to examine the list you just made and find out if there is any recurring theme. Maybe, it is the contribution that keeps coming up, or an effect to seek or give love, or helping your parents cope with old age. Whatever it is, try to identify the central theme of the things you love to do, and try to put these things in a short and precise statement. This will be your 'Mission Statement'. It may even be a quote by a famous person, or a philosophy that has influenced you. Of course, as you grow up, this statement could evolve, but its soul will remain the same. Now, write down your Mission Statement.

Aligning your LIFE with the Underlying Principle:

The final step in this journey is to map your path to your ultimate purpose. Make the little changes in your lifestyle that would accommodate this new principle in your life. LIVE this principle each and every day. It might take a few days, but you will certainly feel the difference in your enthusiasm for life. If you realize that you love being amidst nature, plan out your holiday in a place that will accommodate your new love. Maybe an outing with your children could be enough to recoup with your energy. On the other hand, you might even want to change your job, or start a new business, that is more in line with your mission.

Remember – "Do what you love, and money will follow"

3 Simple Keys to Getting Rid of Fear

Fear doesn't help you, it hinders you. Fear doesn't get you through an open door; it keeps you outside in the hallway. Fear never helps you put your best foot forward; it just keeps both of your feet in cement. You can, and will, live without fear.

Fear is your enemy – no other way to describe it. I'm not talking about that natural life preserving action along with a major boost of adrenaline that happens if a wild animal is coming at you. I'm talking about the fears people live with day in and day out.

Someone once described fear as, "Sand in the machinery of life." Fear doesn't help you, it hinders you. Fear doesn't get you through an open door; it keeps you in the hallway. Fear never helps you put your best foot forward; it just keeps both of your feet in cement.

The psychology of today is, "Learn to live with your fears", "Embrace your fears", "It's normal to have fears – everybody does."

It's true; lots of people do have fears. And there are people who are trying to learn how to live with their fears, and embrace them.

But if it's "normal" to have fears, then why would the Bible talk about being delivered from all your fears?

Think about it - if it's normal to have fears, and you had no fears, then you would be abnormal, right? Well why would God want you to be abnormal?

He doesn't. He truly desires for you to be set free from all your fears.

There are many facets and aspects of fear. One of the big ones is having fear of what others think of you. People do things, say things, and even buy things because of the fear that they have of what others think.

Many times people join clubs or organizations because they are afraid that if they don't, others might think badly of them. They have a need to 'fit in'.

People say things and talk a certain way because they are afraid that they might not say the right thing in front of the right people.

People purchase things they don't need because of a fear of not measuring up to those around them. And on and on it goes.

You don't have to live with fear. Here are 3 simple keys to getting rid of fear.

First, start by realizing that God truly loves you and that His love for you is unconditional. Dwelling on this will give you comfort. The Bible teaches that nothing can separate you from His love. Nothing at all, ever. His love for you does not change, ever!

Second, ask God to help you to get rid of all your fears. He has promised to deliver you from all your fears. That is His desire for you – a life without fear.

Third, make decisions based on what is best for you, and only you, not how it may or may not appear to others. You'll never, ever be able to please everyone, so stop trying to. You'll never, ever be right in everybody's eyes, so it's best to stop trying to.

When you make a decision, ask yourself, "Why am I making this decision? Is it based on fear?" Make decisions based on what is right and best for your life, regardless of what others think.

You can live without fear.

Five practical tips for starting a great conversation in a group situation.

Starting a conversation is not always easy. Especially when you don't feel comfortable with the people you are conversing with.

There may well be a very eerie feeling of awkwardness right at the start of the interaction, unless you know the five secrets...

Here are five secrets to starting a great conversation with a group of people:

1. Get everyone involved.

When starting a conversation, introducing people to each other could be necessary. That is if you don´t know each other or some of those present don´t.

Then, connect one of your group to the topic you are talking about by inviting him to contribute. Or you might simply relate one person to another with their commonalities to encourage dialogue.

2. Choose a topic.

When starting your conversation, choose a general topic. One that everyone can relate to. This will let everyone feel that they belong. This is a great way to encourage everyone to share ideas.

3. Do not drill a person with questions.

This should be avoided especially when asking one person only. The person may feel that he or she is facing a firing squad. Asking too many questions to a person may let him or her feel uncomfortable.

By doing so you might give that person a reason to leave the conversation. The others may also feel uncomfortable with this - they might think that they will be asked next!

4. Break the ice.

At first, there may be awkwardness among the group. You can work to break the ice. Each one of the members is just waiting for someone to do this. You can do this by cracking a joke to make them laugh. You can also start by telling a story. This may lead them to share their story, too. Then, everything will follow.

5. Ask open-ended questions.

These require a more than yes or no answer. These questions will make the flow of your conversation much smoother if done intelligently. These questions can even lead you to another topic.

Asking questions allows you to quickly test the waters to see which topics people are interested in discussing. Just be careful to ask with a pleasing tone.

It is not necessary that you use all of these tips or to use them in order. You can simply choose which ones are most appropriate for the situations you find yourself in. What matters is using these tips to kick off a conversation on a positive upbeat tone.

Once you start experimenting with new ways to start conversations you will notice what works best for your personality. At this point it will all be much easier and before you know it you may even enjoy meeting new people.

The next step is to examine the list you just made and find out if there is any recurring theme. Maybe, it is the contribution that keeps coming up, or an effect to seek or give love, or helping your parents cope with old age. Whatever it is, try to identify the central theme of the things you love to do, and try to put these things in a short and precise statement. This will be your 'Mission Statement'. It may even be a quote by a famous person, or a philosophy that has influenced you. Of course, as you grow up, this statement could evolve, but its soul will remain the same. Now, write down your Mission Statement.

Aligning your LIFE with the Underlying Principle:

The final step in this journey is to map your path to your ultimate purpose. Make the little changes in your lifestyle that would accommodate this new principle in your life. LIVE this principle each and every day. It might take a few days, but you will certainly feel the difference in your enthusiasm for life. If you realize that you love being amidst nature, plan out your holiday in a place that will accommodate your new love. Maybe an outing with your children could be enough to recoup with your energy. On the other hand, you might even want to change your job, or start a new business, that is more in line with your mission.

Remember – "Do what you love, and money will follow"

3 Simple Keys to Getting Rid of Fear

Fear doesn't help you, it hinders you. Fear doesn't get you through an open door; it keeps you outside in the hallway. Fear never helps you put your best foot forward; it just keeps both of your feet in cement. You can, and will, live without fear.

Fear is your enemy – no other way to describe it. I'm not talking about that natural life preserving action along with a major boost of adrenaline that happens if a wild animal is coming at you. I'm talking about the fears people live with day in and day out.

Someone once described fear as, "Sand in the machinery of life." Fear doesn't help you, it hinders you. Fear doesn't get you through an open door; it keeps you in the hallway. Fear never helps you put your best foot forward; it just keeps both of your feet in cement.

The psychology of today is, "Learn to live with your fears", "Embrace your fears", "It's normal to have fears – everybody does."

It's true; lots of people do have fears. And there are people who are trying to learn how to live with their fears, and embrace them.

But if it's "normal" to have fears, then why would the Bible talk about being delivered from all your fears?

Think about it - if it's normal to have fears, and you had no fears, then you would be abnormal, right? Well why would God want you to be abnormal?

He doesn't. He truly desires for you to be set free from all your fears.

There are many facets and aspects of fear. One of the big ones is having fear of what others think of you. People do things, say things, and even buy things because of the fear that they have of what others think.

Many times people join clubs or organizations because they are afraid that if they don't, others might think badly of them. They have a need to 'fit in'.

People say things and talk a certain way because they are afraid that they might not say the right thing in front of the right people.

People purchase things they don't need because of a fear of not measuring up to those around them. And on and on it goes.

You don't have to live with fear. Here are 3 simple keys to getting rid of fear.

First, start by realizing that God truly loves you and that His love for you is unconditional. Dwelling on this will give you comfort. The Bible teaches that nothing can separate you from His love. Nothing at all, ever. His love for you does not change, ever!

Second, ask God to help you to get rid of all your fears. He has promised to deliver you from all your fears. That is His desire for you – a life without fear.

Third, make decisions based on what is best for you, and only you, not how it may or may not appear to others. You'll never, ever be able to please everyone, so stop trying to. You'll never, ever be right in everybody's eyes, so it's best to stop trying to.

When you make a decision, ask yourself, "Why am I making this decision? Is it based on fear?" Make decisions based on what is right and best for your life, regardless of what others think.

You can live without fear.

Five practical tips for starting a great conversation in a group situation.

Starting a conversation is not always easy. Especially when you don't feel comfortable with the people you are conversing with.

There may well be a very eerie feeling of awkwardness right at the start of the interaction, unless you know the five secrets...

Here are five secrets to starting a great conversation with a group of people:

1. Get everyone involved.

When starting a conversation, introducing people to each other could be necessary. That is if you don't know each other or some of those present don't.

Then, connect one of your group to the topic you are talking about by inviting him to contribute. Or you might simply relate one person to another with their commonalities to encourage dialogue.

2. Choose a topic.

When starting your conversation, choose a general topic. One that everyone can relate to. This will let everyone feel that they belong. This is a great way to encourage everyone to share ideas.

3. Do not drill a person with questions.

This should be avoided especially when asking one person only. The person may feel that he or she is facing a firing squad. Asking too many questions to a person may let him or her feel uncomfortable.

By doing so you might give that person a reason to leave the conversation. The others may also feel uncomfortable with this - they might think that they will be asked next!

4. Break the ice.

At first, there may be awkwardness among the group. You can work to break the ice. Each one of the members is just waiting for someone to do this. You can do this by cracking a joke to make them laugh. You can also start by telling a story. This may lead them to share their story, too. Then, everything will follow.

5. Ask open-ended questions.

These require a more than yes or no answer. These questions will make the flow of your conversation much smoother if done intelligently. These questions can even lead you to another topic.

Asking questions allows you to quickly test the waters to see which topics people are interested in discussing. Just be careful to ask with a pleasing tone.

It is not necessary that you use all of these tips or to use them in order. You can simply choose which ones are most appropriate for the situations you find yourself in. What matters is using these tips to kick off a conversation on a positive upbeat tone.

Once you start experimenting with new ways to start conversations you will notice what works best for your personality. At this point it will all be much easier and before you know it you may even enjoy meeting new people.

8 A GIFT OF ENERGY

That sounds great, doesn't it?

Couldn't we all use a little more energy from time to time? I know I could. Right now, for instance, as I sit with a blanket over my shoulders, sipping lemon tea and hoping that the next coughing spasm is not as ferocious as the last two, I could use a gift of energy. The tickle that started in my nose and chest a few days ago has blossomed into a full-blown, body-wracking cold, complete with chills and fever.

The martial art Aikido (The Way of Harmony) teaches us to see everything that comes our way as energy to be danced with. By centering and extending our ki (life energy) we connect and blend with the energy of attack, making it a part of us. We redirect it from the center, keeping ourselves and our family safe from harm.

How this elegant metaphor applies to situations in our personal and professional lives is a continuing source of study and fascination for me. One of the ways I work at integrating Aiki principles into my life is by sharing the philosophy with other people. My workshops use physical exercises which help our bodies to remember how to do things we have forgotten, things like center, extend, acknowledge and blend. We begin to dance, flow and move with the energy of conflict instead of blocking it.

So I sit, wondering how I can dance with this attack. Even centering doesn't stop the incessant coughing. I have no ki to extend (it seems to have retreated to the innermost recesses of my system). The only thing I can think to do is to acknowledge and embrace.

But that, at least, is a beginning. In years past, I would not acknowledge being sick. When I was sick, I'd often go to work anyway. I plowed through what needed doing with half a spirit and wore myself out. I probably infected half a dozen others in the process. I was sometimes ill-tempered, depressed and depressing to be around. If I can't acknowledge what's going on, whether it's a cold or a problem at home, I surely can't embrace it. By this I mean make it a part of me, connect with it so that I can begin to look for solutions.

Most of our conflicts, internal or external, would resolve themselves if we would only take this first step - acknowledge them! But because we see them as negative, we immediately resist by fighting or fleeing. If I can see what comes my way as energy, with no positive or negative charge other than what I give it, I can be more curious about it. As unwanted as it may be, there's definitely more power in dancing with it than in resisting it.

As for my cold, I'm still trying to learn if there's a gift here somewhere. Let's see - I've already read a book I've been putting aside for months, started another, and gotten some much needed rest (in between coughs!). I may not always know what the energy offers, but when I can ask the question "Where's the gift?" I've taken a first, important, step in a new direction.

Don't Be a Victim of the People Pleasing Quadrant.

People pleasing can be a defeating habit in a person's life, simply because the act itself takes your focus off what you CAN control, and puts your focus on what you CAN'T control, which is somebody else's happiness and peace of mind. Here is a perfect example to illustrate my point

If you buy your lover flowers, and they come home to tell you they just received a raise at work – the flowers you give them are just going to add to their joy, and you are going to have a wonderful evening.

However, if you buy your lover flowers, and they come home to tell you they just got fired from work – they may look at the flowers and give a quick smile just to acknowledge you and quickly go back to sulking – or worse, they may be hateful and yell, "WHAT GOOD ARE FLOWERS GOING TO DO ME NOW?!?!? ARE THEY HIRING FLORISTS?!?!"

Of course, this is common sense – but it is a perfect example of why people pleasing doesn't work 100% of the time. You will never be able to predict what kind of mood anyone is going to be in all the time, simply because things will always happen outside of our control. Consequently, your happiness or misery is in the other person's hands, which puts you into a very vulnerable position.

I have developed what I call, "The People Pleasing Quadrant" to broaden readers' awareness of what people-pleasing is, and what to do once those people-pleasing tendencies rear their ugly heads. Quadrant means "four" which means there are four different situations you will find yourself in that you will need to develop strategies to combat your people-pleasing tendencies. The four situations are as follows:

Quadrant # 1: Dealing with the people you like or love when those people ALSO like or love you in return:

This first quadrant is the easiest to manage, because at least you genuinely like or love the person you are dealing with, and they like or love you as well. However, remember the example we used above about the lover losing their job and the flowers? No matter how much you like or love someone, or how much they like or love you, bad things happen sometimes. We all say things we don't mean. The trick is to not take the people you care about personally, and feel responsible for "fixing" them. Let the person you like and love be hurt, angry, mad, and upset. It doesn't have to affect your core happiness, although you can sympathize with the person and let them know you will be there for them, if they want to talk.

Besides, this person cares about you – and they don't want to drag you down, just because they are having a bad day. Give them a little space, and let things sort themselves out. Spend your energy focusing on more productive ventures, such as going for a jog to get in shape, studying for an important test, or reading a book that is of interest to you. People-pleasing is really annoying to people who like or love you already. They don't expect you to make everything better, they just need some time to get over it.

Quadrant # 2: Dealing with the people you like or love when those people DON'T like or love you in return:

The second quadrant is oftentimes the most painful quadrant to come to terms with, regardless if it is about a "friend," family member, or lover. Once in a great while, we can like or even love someone who doesn't like or love us in return. We do everything in our power to be "good" enough, "supportive" enough, "encouraging" enough, "kind" enough, whatever enough! But somehow, it is never enough, and it never will be.

Once in a while, these people we like or love are nice to us out of pity, guilt, regret or remorse – or because we are fulfilling some kind of need for them that they don't want to give up. Don't mistake their temporary kindness as genuine concern! Because honestly, these people don't like or love us at all. It could be for a variety of reasons, but those reasons don't have anything to do with you.

The trick for getting over people-pleasing in this quadrant is to realize what quadrant these people belong in, and come to terms with the fact that they don't like or love you. On the other hand, realize that there are millions of other people out here who would absolutely adore you. Realize that you are wasting your valuable and precious time with people pleasing, especially in this quadrant, because no matter what you do, it won't matter. Just move on to someone who will like, love and appreciate the beautiful person you are.

Quadrant # 3: Dealing with the people you DON'T like or love, when those people DO like or love you.

Most of the people-pleasing in this quadrant comes out of guilt, pity or personal gain. Although I must admit, it is really hard not to like someone who likes you, but you may be able to definitely see that the other person likes or loves you WAY more than you like or love them.

I believe my grandmother taught me a very gracious lesson about how to handle situations in quadrant three. One day, a boy who just moved into my neighborhood decided to ask me out on a date. He really had a crush on me, and I could tell. However, I didn't feel the same way about him. But I did enjoy all of the flowers, candy and attention he gave me.

At the time, I didn't see anything wrong with taking whatever he was willing to give. But my grandmother pulled me aside and told me why it wasn't nice to encourage gestures and lead a person on, especially when I knew his intentions. Of course, I liked him as a person because he was so sweet. But the truth of the matter is, he was wasting his time courting me when I wasn't interested.

Although I could have continued to use him, I went with granny's advice and politely told him that I could no longer accept gifts because I was not interested in dating anyone at that time. However, we decided to be friends and did fun things together on occasion. He found a new girlfriend who truly adored him to pieces, and fell in love with her. The last I heard, they were planning to get married. The moral of the story is, he was a sweetheart, and deserved to find someone who liked and loved him. It would be selfish of me to stand in the way of that.

Quadrant # 4: Dealing with the people you DON'T like when they DON'T like you either!

A person will rarely find themselves in this quadrant when it comes to their personal life, unless it has to do with Ex-Lovers or step families. Otherwise, you can just get up and walk away, which is why quadrant four is reserved mostly for the workplace and figures of authority!

People-pleasing in this quadrant reflects suppressed feelings, and putting up with a lot of emotional, mental and verbal abuse. It can be because you are afraid of losing your job or because you are afraid of the person themselves. In situations like this, it is always best to get a third party involved, because for one reason or another – you are forced to deal with this person, and they are forced to deal with you. Neither one of you is going to be able to compromise about a reasonable solution on your own, because both of you don't care what is in the other's best interest! There needs to be a mediator who can look at the situation objectively on neutral ground, and come up with a reasonable solution.

Don't be afraid to be the bigger person and ask for outside help. It is the only way the conflict will be resolved. In matters dealing with the family, it may be best to go to counseling, join a support group, or bring a person from the outside into the situation. Remember, your goal is to conserve energy, and focus on how you can change things, and make them head in a positive direction. Be a part of the solution, not the problem. If everyone else wants to wallow in their misery and problems, you can let them do just that. But you can choose something different.

In closing, when you eliminate people pleasing in your life for good – it is always great to have the awareness that you only have a one in four shot of really hitting it off with somebody special! (In case you were wondering, that one shot lies within people who are in Quadrant number one!) If you go into each situation expecting the

best, but prepared for the worse – you will always come out on top. But most importantly, be yourself! There is no point going through life pretending to think and feel a certain way just to please other people. Besides that, you won't have the opportunity to attract the people in your life who would really like or love the person you truly are!

Another tidbit I'd like to share out of granny's little treasure chest of knowledge, wisdom and experience. She always used to say, "Rhiannon, there are three types of people in this world. There are givers and there are takers. But once in a great while, you will be fortunate enough to find a person who is capable of doing both."

I hope this article will encourage you to be a person who can do both.

5 Powerful Reasons Why INSPIRATION Should Be a Part of YOUR Success Strategy

Let's face it. Life can be difficult. It just can be. Work pressures mount, family demands become overwhelming, health suffers, stress builds.

I have to admit, it happens to me and when it does, when life gets to be too much or too hard, I put up a "CLOSED for business" sign and seek out a little inspiration.

Inspiration looks good (a beautiful photograph), smells good (a bed of roses), sounds good (Vivaldi's Four Seasons) and feels good (family photographs, your favorite movie or book).

Surrounding yourself with inspiration helps you get and keep your life on track because it returns you to YOUR spirit – to your center. When you feel inspired, it's a sign you're touching a place deep within yourself. From this place, you can create, plan, and simply live a life that feels better. And when you feel better, everything runs a bit more smoothly, creativity increases, things get done, you feel happier.

1. Inspiration is Heart Opening. Think about the last time you read an inspiring story. Did your heart feel 10 times bigger than normal? Inspiration opens your heart and when your heart is open you become more accepting of yourself and others. You feel more patient. Your general outlook improves. Connecting with your heart reduces stress.

2. Inspiration Inspires Greatness. Have you ever seen a beautiful

painting and had the urge to stop by your nearest art supply store for a canvas and oil paints? Inspiring works of art touch within us our innate desire to create art that's unique to us. (art = an outward expression of your deepest joy)

3. Inspiration Calms and Restores Nature. Fresh air. Wide open spaces. Sunny, hot beaches. Don't you already feel more relaxed? Exactly! Mother Nature is ready and willing to share her inspired works of art with us. She's made it highly accessible and totally free!

4. Inspiration Energizes and Refreshes. How did you feel watching Lance Armstrong win the Tour de France for the 7th time? Did it make you want to jump on your bike for a 2400 hundred mile bike ride on steep mountain roads? Maybe! Did it make you want to do something greater with your life? Inspiration is powerful because it touches the part of us that knows, deep inside, we're made for so much more.

5. Inspiration Spreads Joy. Inspiration makes you feel good. Just think of the last inspiring chain-email you received and passed on with a note that said, "I never do this but I had to share this with you!" When you feel good, when the joy in you comes alive, and you share your joy with others, you impact the world in a thousand positive ways.

The next time life feels difficult, put up a "CLOSED for business" sign and get out for a little inspiration. You'll love the results

9 APPRECIATE YOURSELF & WHAT YOU HAVE

A better life has been achieved when we are no longer trying to achieve a better life. It means that we are content, as we should be, with ourselves and what we have. To be anxious for more or to envy someone else's life or possessions is self-defeating. We are then in a constant state of frustration, always hoping and waiting for more happiness.

So what is important? Enough, not more.

"Think of what you have rather than of what you lack. Of the things you have, select the best and then reflect how eagerly you would have sought them if you did not have them." - Marcus Aurelius.

There is, here and now, much to appreciate. There is life itself with friends, family, and everything that is naturally before us. We just have to look around and take it in. Perhaps it is time to make a list of all the good things we have to be grateful for.

Are there people in your life that you would miss dearly if they were not here? When you go for a walk don't you see, hear, and smell, many things to appreciate and feel nice about? Like the flowers, trees, birds, and the clouds in the sky. A caterpillar crossing the sidewalk or your neighbor waving. A cute pup or child enthusiastically enjoying that moment in life.

"Whether in favor or in humiliation, be not dismayed. Let your eyes leisurely look at the flowers blooming and falling in your courtyard. Whether you leave or retain your position, take no care. Let your mind wander with the clouds folding and unfolding beyond the horizon." - Hung Tzu-ch'eng (1593-1665)

It just makes good sense to be satisfied and at peace with yourself and others, and to enjoy life now.

ABOUT THE AUTHOR

Lynnie Ceniza has lived and worked in four different countries in her short life. She is now settled in the United Kingdom with her husband and son. She has learned to be positive - less stressed.

She has supported her elderly parents all her working life - and she still does. She is the sole breadwinner for her elderly parents in the Philippines. The hard times and troubles have made her strong and determined, and given her a really positive attitude. Although she is now a full time housewife and a Mother, she still has time for her hobby, photography, and loves to share her work. She believes that being a positive thinker helps with stress management and can improve health.

Lynnie is aiming to help people who need support and suicidal awareness. She loves charity work, She has experienced and suffered depression and anxiety and now she will share with you the power of positivity, she supports all her friends emotionally when they feel alone and sad.

* Studied Positive Thinking Life Coach Training Accredited Certification Positive Thinking Life

*PROMOTING POSITIVE BEHAVIOUR CERTIFICATE

Life is beautiful, enjoy it while you can ☺

Made in the USA
Coppell, TX
07 March 2021